Me Counting Time

by Joan Sweeney · illustrated by Alex Willmore

Alfred A. Knopf · New York

For my brothers, Ed and Jim,
who gave me the answers I needed just in time! —J.S.

For Dara and Walter —A.W.

THIS IS A BORZOI BOOK PUBLISHED BY ALFRED A. KNOPF

Text copyright © 2000 by Joan Sweeney
Cover art and interior illustrations copyright © 2019 by Alex Willmore

Visit us on the Web! rhcbooks.com

Educators and librarians, for a variety of teaching tools, visit us at
RHTeachersLibrarians.com

Library of Congress Cataloging-in-Publication Data is available upon request.

ISBN 978-0-525-64684-6 (trade) — ISBN 978-0-525-64685-3 (pbk.) — ISBN 978-0-525-64686-0 (ebook)

The text of this book is set in 20-point New Century Schoolbook LT Pro.
The illustrations were drawn in pencil, then scanned and colored digitally.

MANUFACTURED IN CHINA
August 2019
10 9 8 7 6 5 4 3 2 1
2019 Knopf Books for Young Readers Edition

This is me. I'm inviting my friends to my
birthday party. I'm going to be seven years old.

Just think—seven candles for seven years. But a year isn't a candle, a year is a measurement of time.

Time comes in different amounts—seconds, minutes, hours, days, and more. Here's how I tell them apart.

First I think of the blink of an eye. That's about one second of time. I can count seconds by saying "one Mississippi, two Mississippi."

Then I think of *sixty seconds*. That's one minute of time. I can write an invitation to my party in one minute!

Then I think of *sixty minutes*. That's one hour of time—the time it takes to make a birthday cake!

Then I think of *twenty-four hours*. That's one day.
The earth rotates once every day.

Then I think of *seven days*.
That's one week.

MONDAY

TUESDAY

WEDNESDAY

THURSDAY

FRIDAY

SATURDAY

SUNDAY

Then I think of *four weeks*. That's about one month.
Most months are just over four weeks. Only February
is four weeks *exactly*—except during leap year. Then
it's four weeks plus one day!

Then I think of *twelve months*. That's one year.
From winter to spring to summer to fall.

1 YEAR

2 YEARS

3 YEARS

4 YEARS

5 YEARS

6 YEARS

7 YEARS

8 YEARS

9 YEARS

10 YEARS

Then I think of *ten years*. Ten years is called a decade—
even longer than I've been alive.

And then I think of *ten decades*. One hundred years.
That's one century. Long enough for a tree to grow
real tall.

A CASTLE BUILT IN THE YEAR 1000

SAND CASTLE, VIRGINIA BEACH 2019

Then I think of *ten centuries*. That's the same as one millennium. One thousand years!

Imagine. 31,557,600,000 blinks of an eye! That's a long, long time.

A lot longer than seven years! So how do I get from a millennium to my time? From a millennium to *now*? Here's how.

A **millennium** ago, someone built a Viking ship like this.
Now it would be one thousand years—ten centuries—old!
A **century** ago, my great-great-grandpa had this picture
taken. Now it's one hundred years old.

A **decade** ago, my nana sewed this wedding dress for my mother. Now it's ten years old.

A **year** ago, my family moved to our brand-new house. Now it's twelve months old.

About a **month** ago, my cat had kittens.
Now they're four weeks old.

A **week** ago, I got new soccer shoes.
Now they're seven days old.

A **day** ago, I painted this picture.
Now it's twenty-four hours old.

1 MILLENNIUM

1 CENTURY

1 DECADE

1 YEAR

My dad can make my birthday cake in one **hour**.
An **hour** is sixty minutes. A **minute** is sixty seconds.
And a **second** is like the blink of an eye.

In seven days, I'll be seven years old. Seven candles.
220,838,400 blinks of an eye!

I can't wait for my party. I'm going to have the time of my life!

TIME

60 seconds = 1 minute

60 minutes = 1 hour

24 hours = 1 day

7 days = 1 week

4 weeks = about 1 month

12 months = 1 year

10 years = 1 decade

100 years = 1 century

10 centuries = 1 millennium